IN A LANGUAGE
THAT YOU KNOW

Len Verwey

University of Nebraska Press / Lincoln and London

Acknowledgments for the use of copyrighted
material appear on page 55, which constitutes
an extension of the copyright page.

The African Poetry Book Series has been made
possible through the generosity of philanthropists
Laura and Robert F. X. Sillerman, whose
contributions have facilitated the establishment
and operation of the African Poetry Book Fund.

Library of Congress Cataloging-in-Publication Data
Names: Verwey, Len, author.
Title: In a language that you know / Len Verwey.
Description: Lincoln: University of Nebraska
Press, [2017] | Series: African Poetry Book
series | Includes bibliographical references.
Identifiers: LCCN 2017003731 (print)
LCCN 2017008050 (ebook)
ISBN 9780803290983 (softcover: acid-free paper)
ISBN 9781496203175 (epub)
ISBN 9781496203182 (mobi)
ISBN 9781496203199 (pdf)
Classification: LCC PR9369.4.V49 A6 2017 (print)
LCC PR9369.4.V49 (ebook) | DDC 823/.92—dc23
LC record available at
https://lccn.loc.gov/2017003731

Set in Garamond Premier by Rachel Gould.
Designed by N. Putens.

IN A LANGUAGE THAT YOU KNOW

African
POETRY
BOOK SERIES

Series editor: Kwame Dawes

CONTENTS

IN A LANGUAGE THAT YOU KNOW

Coast

It is just habit or superstition,
it keeps nothing at bay and no one safe,
yet each time heavy weather moves in

they chant the same old words
under their breath
and carefully count the boats pulled up
on the sand and fastened to the stone.

As though they didn't know exactly
who was back on land,
who still wasn't.

As though any fool couldn't see
that the flimsy boats of husbands and fathers
do not stand
a chance, should the winter ocean
bring its full flexing strength around.

As though the shuffling
walk to the cottage and the apartment block,
the refusal to look back harbor-ward,
the slurping at the tea with the
wind-slammed rain at the window all night

constituted magic,
and magic enough to alter, this time,
the trajectory of those
as good as dead out there.

We children whisper too
from behind our hands
as though something catching were in the air.

Perhaps we are quick learners,
clever as orphans,
but more likely it is just how
we play, a secret giggle in it, a mockery even,

being tired of the warnings and
the tatty clippings from the local paper,
this living as though there is a war
when there isn't a war.

Better to go out early after storms,
the householders asleep, the air
so closely punctured
anything might shine through,

to take the dogs and a hat and see
what debris has been left for one,
better to sing
the songs with water in them.

My Mother Speaks

Lorenço Marques, 1973.
Speaking no Portuguese, in all my labor
I could not make myself understood,
and your father would not be hauled
from where he smoked to view
this thing happening, the body ground away
sheer as ribbon then stretched bone to bone
to make a passing.
So in silence I delivered.

First child, I wanted you quick, your smell
on me before the world's on you,
but they brought you cleaned and weighed,
they'd fixed you up and stitched me up
as though we needed them
to be lovely for each other.

You never asked about your birth.
In the backyard tree you lived, a halfway bird
perched in shorts above the suburb's barking dogs,
what boyish vow or test had you imposed now,
I wondered, thinking soon you'd tell,
but every year you spoke less to me or anyone
and walked in wider circles around my love.

Whatever else you may have thought, or think now,
dear son what was wrong with me
and us is wrong with you also,
your silence my silence,
something else that will not move and cannot flinch,
even as you screamed later at the needle going in

or the tooth coming out, the ragged bone
pinned all wrong beneath the skin,
even as you huddled
with the curious men inside the shed,
to watch them hood and castrate the farmer's roaming dog,
and how he bled, even as
you bleakly trumpeted your longing and your anger
in the manner of the time.

Women know what's nonsense and know what
cannot be hoped for, and so do you,
a mother's son through and through,
even as you left,
even as a perched small boy
on the night ridges where I'd never been,
where the helicopters, even then,
silver-sprayed the veld around you,
looking for bandits and secrets.

Fishing Boy

Wading knee-deep through the surf,
unreeling as they return
they cast his line and theirs.

It is understood
he lacks technique and strength
to do it for himself, to get beyond
the banked sand to the big ones,
but he scans the water as they do,
wills the fish to hook like them.

Holiday fishermen.
Yet with dry knowing laughter
at those who bait big
only to cast short, a fleshy strength,
the certainty that what they know of tide
and current and seasonal movement
will serve them well
enough as it has before.

While he holds a lucky stone
secretly in his free hand,
lights their cigarettes for them without inhaling,
a boy, what he has
next to nothing, what he wills more
a desperate miracle:

that if the line should
jerk he may rear and pull until his fish lies
gasping dying silver on the sand,
may pull his hands to blood

for such a fact
on this beach under this sky
and then the victorious procession,

the erect little solemn Caesar
back to the womenfolk
on the beach house balcony,
the brown light legs and summer
dress of the cousin, the sip of beer
offered by the father, every other fishing boy
awed into wondering silence,

the story with him in it
and the catch to back it up.

Fathers to Sons

You huddle together though it is not cold,
most serious, most amusing when you ask for
more and better information.

And perhaps you are right to ask us, old men
who do not blink, nibbling at
our food, coughing at night,
but a kind of vigil in us still,
a gauntness not so different from yours.

And our city also your home,
flung bones
you cannot read the pattern of.

Keep your snot-noses to the chill windowpane,
we might say, wait for a beam
to sweep across you, some night
much like this, if you like.
It would have to be night.

It cannot hurt, and we promise not to laugh
when we see you trample one another,
eager for that light,
or to wrist-flick
all the beautiful machinery
that makes it to hell and gone.

The rules do not permit it, for one,
and we are not sure we could,
but we wouldn't
put it past us to let you sleep,
if you were to sleep.

To shake at you later, after the fact,
in sympathy as it were, then to say
listen, you could still catch the last of it

but come stand with us instead,
come look here
where again it is morning.

Bitter Boys

Whose own mother left them
three years ago, whose father cares for them now
though barely, it is said, always ill-fitting
school uniforms and dirty casual clothes,
who do no sports, and owning nothing
are impossible to punish.

The school and the suburb knows it.
Too young for banishment they must
be accommodated yet might run amok,
say *we couldn't help ourselves,*
mutilation's in our blood.

How could they, motherless, ever know
which versions of themselves should
take precedence? How could they learn
to want what it is possible to have?

In the rain my mother drives me to school but
there they are at the bus stop, moping
in regulation school-gray rain jackets.
A lift can't be offered, consider their likely *wetness*
and their intractable
group lumpiness, the three of them
dripping there in the backseats,
struggling with seat belts
and where to put their bags,
and the dank smell of them in the tight car.

Would they speak in unison, like angels?
Would they have a chosen speaker, and if so

would they confer before responding?
In whispers or by silent looks?

Or would they speak independently in strange grunts,
produce a chaotic babble that
could not be quieted?

It is inexplicable, how they keep to themselves,
how quietly they play, serious
and strong-shouldered and ineffectual as birds,
even now by the canal, as though unobserved,
unhated, as though they will not die of bullets and
fast moving cars and needles
in rooms in other cities, scattered,
die of their own sheer unbelonging
the way I would if I were them.

El Bandito de los Nadas

Weighing almost nothing that summer
I climbed the Pyrenees on my silver bicycle,
master of the surprise breakaway,

the sun-sheeted roads and the
noise of fans and motorcycles and helicopters
always accompanying us,

every start and finish town with
its fat mayor and dingy hotel rooms,
my thirst and the dust in everything,

and the doubters said *too far from the finish*
as I accelerated, but I won
more often than I lost, proclaimed

from the podiums in my broken Spanish
that I was uncatchable
when I was in form, and the price seemed reasonable,

a universe of wanting without humor
or mercy, a youth dazed by heavy training,
strange hours and little friendship,

a mother and father crying
even after I returned
with prizes and gifts.

The Quarry

There one of us dived and didn't surface.
Perhaps he hit his head.
Perhaps there was an underwater ledge.

They searched the evening and the night,
the bumbling adults
of that place, searched their
goldless ghost town for the hero,

who perhaps had pushed aside
the rock, bored,
intent on a modest local fame,

and chuckled down there later
when the serious council
fenced the quarry,
put up warning signs,

and the rest of us swam regardless
many afternoons.

Old Joke

Old joke, always long in the telling,
a cancer-dead uncle told
when I was a boy and everyone got together:
December holidays, beach house,
sun and water, white living.

About a letter or a slip of paper, its meaning
impenetrable to its carrier,
that nonetheless destroyed everything
between himself
and the people he showed it to.

He doggedly kept showing it,
he didn't learn,
and so he lost it all in time—
family, friends, love, money,
they seemed to understand
the contents, he didn't, until his life
was just the
search for explanation.

Eventually he found an old man
down by a harbor (he was old himself)
and the harbor ancient
knew and was willing to tell.

But then the breeze lifts the paper
at the last possible moment,
sinks it in the gray ocean,
or in some variants the ancient croaks

as he is about to speak,
the outcome the same
whatever the ending,
the listeners always aghast
at the loss, indignant at the escape artistry,

pestering the sly bemused uncle to disclose
the exact words
that could rend so much,
to hand the piece of paper over
if in fact he told
the incomplete story of himself.

For he'd traveled, and was famous
for his bad luck, and only recently
he'd been welcomed to
these gatherings again.

Doubtless he went along
with it to add an extra spice
to a telling
he must've grown tired of,
liked the speculation and the
whispers that followed him around.

And not one of us eager
bright-eyed lads
hesitated to say we'd claim that letter,
did not then and there desire a life
such as the one we
agreed he'd had.

What better
than the loss of everything

without guilt, we thought,
good-byes without a trail of bodies,
words that release
and cannot be understood
but almost can.

The Bills

She says any pill might
help but none will help for certain.
We are familiar with her crafty vagueness,
her disfigured age, the wind around her quarters
that turns the blades
and churns the red mud continuously.

We are not surprised that it is always dusk,
that she must strain without her spectacles
to read the writing on the labels,
turn and hold the ampoules to the
little light, or make a call from memories
of what she gave before.

We know too that she will file
her fingernails and wait us out
when we demand
apology for an error that she's made,
what she gives only given to keep us coming anyway,
rarely more than she can get away with,
taken only in believing this time
round her usual rules will not apply,
or at least not for a month or two
until the bills come due.

The Real Evidence

Cops are easily charmed
by the unexplaining unrepentant killer.
A nudge a wink and they arrest the fool
next door (they like a good joke
when the mood is on them),
and I'm sipping hot chocolate in bed,
happy, gun now hot now cold under
the covers with me, tut-tutting
with the neighbors in the morning,
thinking next time I might call
the ambulance myself, tell them
not to hurry, don't bother,
though that might give the game away.
Though nothing seems to give the game away.

Someone somewhere, not an ordinary cop,
must have all the evidence already,
the real evidence,
must be waiting with the pictures
and the recordings of conversations and the traces of me
on objects, I wasn't that careful,
must have watched me all these years
when I fooled the others, who had it coming,
as do I of course, as does he no doubt,
though he'll laugh politely
when I say I need some time to think,
unworried, decorous, implacable,
there's little he doesn't see. Always already
on his way to collecting me.

Campaign

We set off and return in grayness, pass
the growing animal entourage that
sleeps curled against the perimeter wire,
close as it can manage to our fires.

The severed heads poled along the highway:
a leering puppetry,
fitted to the dim-dawned place we've made.
Only the very old and very young
in the villages we raze.

Our generals sleep soundly, without exception,
wake slowly
to their coffee in the morning.

Nights I have stood outside my tent, seen
the orange glow far across the dark space
ringing the plateau, yet felt the heat on my skin,
felt that I could fan the flames from
where I stood, if I wanted.

I concluded nothing then.
To think too far along such lines,
while others sleep, is to risk everything.

We torched the maps
when we torched the crops.
We torched the crops
when we knew those back home
wouldn't take us in again.

The maps meant nothing anyway.

Experts

We come for information.
We come by order, otherwise
we would not come.

Here, in settlements like this, the
secret leaders lurk, the plans are made,
according to our experts.

If we took them seriously
entire battalions
might be sheltered under us in a
complex of shafts and cells.

The ground might sag beneath us
as we walk
between the corrugated iron shacks,
any floor in any dwelling
lead to guns and beasts, radios
and food, enough to keep
going for a hundred years.

They lack the facts, these experts
of ours, they must guess
and fabulate like us,
who know that we know nothing,
but they do not doubt themselves
and so are inexhaustible.

What we get for our threats
cannot be understood, outpaces
the best of our translators,
and after the bewildered

shrugs come the papers, the array
of useless paper and trinkets
presented solemnly before us,
collected and hauled back
as though we'd finally found
the secret stash.

We collect it all:
rag dolls, handkerchiefs, birth
and death certificates, proofs of immunization,
bills of entry and a poster
of Maradona, a breastfeeding
booklet, a prescription pad,
pages from a novel.

No doubt a kind of revenge, this
thoroughness of ours.
Let the experts lose themselves in it.

The big-eyed children lined against the wall
will kick their gutted ball
as soon as we depart.
The shacks are only shacks,
and the ground solid everywhere we walk.

The Stowaway

I found an agent for such a journey,
to a country where I might work in the
places foreigners can work:
cannery, factory, waitress in a restaurant.

Took my study savings to the man,
his office three plastic chairs and peeling paint.
The rumor was that trawlers,
cargo ships, even yachts would take
you out for money,
but I can't say I was surprised to hear
no tickets were available,
save those reserved for special clients.

There's a war now, you know,
the agent said, and later
shooting off into my mouth,
clamping my head
so I could not move, pawing slide away from me
and I up from the tiles
with a piece of paper.

Out under the harbor wall
the ragged harbor boys casting lines,
somersaulting into the diesel-slicked water,
wondering what I'd earned, stupidly hoping
for a yacht, some abiding movie image
of moonlight on a swell seen from a deck,
when what mattered was only
a dying continent abandoned,
its men and secret bones and war lightning.

Days later we heaved into the swell
in our hidden cabin
in the belly of the trawler, engines churning close to us
where others had come and gone
fearful of being caught, fearing each other
and the loss of precious stones and money and mementos.

In the night the slap of water at the hull,
somebody saying we've stopped, pushing at
the cabin door that opened only from the other side,
as if such effort mattered just as effort,

understanding what I didn't yet,
that the men who entered minutes later
entered from a world whose
every aspect was a thing of theirs,
a sky claimed in all its zones,
any whisper any tremor theirs to use,
bundling us in silence into the van on the quay

of the harbor where we'd started,
ours a sightless cruise, out and back,
the vessel left rocking in its cot of knotted ropes.

Our Leader Speaks

Roads built in my time are once more washed away.
Ministers want stadiums, airports, though poorer
households, connected to the grid, cannot pay.

They liken my rule to a wishful airplane
fallen to real earth, scattering real bodies.

I say the wishful and the whimsical made stone
is the only aim of empire,
and rain cannot rain carefully.

People bear much then tolerate little,
who can say where the knife's edge is?
Aren't we like drunks in a courtyard
who reel, recover,
reel again, insisting all the while on sobriety?

I say every last stadium and airport and clinic may yet be real,
some mix of vision and
delusion may yet out-bluster the networks
against my rule
and the tunnels beneath our city.

The tunnels we used ourselves
when we were the ones in waiting.

Elsewhere

They'll say you are wrong
to think of it as war
when what you saw was
only flailing, half illumined in the flares.

They'll point to problems with the light,
say you cannot trust
the conjuring habit of the hands and eyes
that appear to belie stories of the day.

Under the swinging bulb as figures come and go
the face close to your face
will say the trains now run again,
factories increase
their output, bodies even glisten
on the beach again.

Then later they'll say yes, admittedly our city's
emptied of your friends and colleagues
and the pumps run dry at times, and yes
that was dark smoke
massed above the mall last Saturday.

But how much more ridiculous
you'd seem, huddled on the ice, elsewhere entirely,
with a new name, a fake accent,
clutching photographs that prove or disprove nothing.

And is there not a thrill in knowing that the footage
some will queue to see
is from a neighborhood like yours?

In the sirens and the flags, the beat of helicopter rotors,
the corner men in camouflage?

And you perhaps among the black cars
racing bumper to bumper at dawn
toward the palace?

Leaving

You learned to drink and laugh
with the generals and their dancers,
high in the suite above the poisoned fields
and the paltry linoleum
hosannas of the everyday.

A dream of cold perfection,
a shaded pilot in his bubble.

You came to know the markets within markets
in every city, and opportunities
you'd heard of but didn't think
could possibly exist.

But everything was possible,
and you too haggled
through a half-closed door
for an unchecked night or more.

Take me with you, someone said,
but of course you didn't.

You raced the sand-swept beach roads
back to your apartment,
singing as the tires slipped,
still half erect in that dawn.

Everywhere the failed gods bled
into their failed creations.
It was easy enough to go.

Go, light and fast as a skipping stone,
when what was needed
was the carrying of bones.

Confession of the Stable Hand

I looked after your horses as best I could,
and when you come
to question me, as you must,
I will try to smile,
say that I know nothing almost nothing
of their escape.

I will say I remember little
of the day itself or of the time since then,
and that truthfully
I was alone, there were no other men.

I will say it must have been at night.
I will say they are far from here by now.

When in fact we drew the bolt.

Perhaps they ran
too red eyed, too foam flecked
at the mouth
under too much of a moon-burnt sky.

But it suited them we felt.

I Flew Secretly

I flew secretly, for any side
or any desperate neutral that could meet my fee,

flew at night, self-taught, under my
own instructions and corrections,

learning the tricks that worked, such as a white
ribbon tied to the upper arm.

I would not be caught, my plane so old modern radar
couldn't track me, and slowly slowly I flew,

knowing those on the lookout
would expect me to come in fast and get out fast.

Death, when I imagined it, was capture on the ground,
or drowning entangled in a parachute

while cruel men laughed from a dinghy,
never something that happened in the air.

Inviolate, my spiteful quiet at the earth's curve.
Beautiful, the short-haired clear-eyed woman

afraid of nothing but love and airplanes, who smoked
with me in the vestibules of secret hangars,

sent me on my way, and sometimes
waited for me to get back.

Maputo

I stayed long enough in a sand-floored bar
to confuse a patterned wall
with rippling water, to comment loudly on it
as one does in dreams, then to lose the way
with someone's friend
through market and driftwood shelter,
spilling loosely rolled tobacco as I walked,
unexpected beach and ocean wrapped
around it, and she told me
she wasn't really someone's friend,
was working in fact, and I admitted I didn't handle
drink and fresh air and ocean together
very well, separately it's fine, I said,
and I was broke, financially, admittedly,
though otherwise there had been progress,
and hadn't sailed up
from the south the day before.
Though I would've thought
that part was obvious enough.

An Unchained Dog for Each of You

It is 1995 and you don't know anything.
You probably don't even know yet that you don't know anything.
Which is as it should be.
You are 22, you work as a cashier and you have a friend, a fellow cashier,
a reader of books like you, also thin and ugly, awkward anyway,
and a talker about writing:
the two of you talk far more about writing than you write.
This talking is what you have together
in your drearily concrete northern city,
talk that is love and fear and bravado and
wishing and far-ranging and a honing of the will,
perhaps, a preparation.
Where are your kin? Your teachers?
You have none. You have dead and living
writers and each other, and you tell yourselves
repeatedly that the real writers too were once as you are.
You have so many opinions,
you are so afraid. Your friend
will die seventeen years later of heart failure,
a good death for a writer
as you thought of writers then.
You are often tired in 1995
but they tell you nothing's wrong,
some nights the two of you drive in his
mother's Toyota out through the eastern suburbs
to the gravel roads and
settlements and plots with dogs barking on their chains;
you want to stop and taunt these angry useless dogs
until they are mad
but what if a chain snapped then
and shapes beside the road and

eventually nothing much at all
and you understand and sometimes say to your friend
that if you carried on long enough
in a straight line from here, a night like this,
you'd get to Mozambique, where in fact you were born,
and sometimes you
jump drunk and naked from the roof of his parents' house
into the summer pool, get it wrong and you'll break
your silly neck or back but you don't get it wrong
in 1995, because you don't imagine that you can,
or probably you are just lucky.
His girlfriend jumps too when she's there
and the three of you know
he wants you to touch her in the water
but you are too shy and she is too shy.
One night he puts the car in a ditch, thirty kilometers from home,
and you step into shock night air,
bemused, unhurt, entirely yourselves,
one of you with a bloody face but you don't now remember
who, and all of that back there
to drive back through, but suddenly and for
an instant only
you are precisely where you are.
You should've touched her in the water.
You should've walked into the old land all around
your northern city with blood on your face
and a stupid grin and the tilted car's
front wheel spinning behind you forever,
with your friend's hand in yours, if he wanted to come with,
and an unchained dog for each of you.
You should've walked to
Mozambique making lines of poetry
until someone recognized you for what you were and said,
Welcome, we've waited up for you,

these are your rooms for the night.
You should've stayed, lived by candlelight
and starlight until the search parties gave up,
standing on the dawn *stoep* wrapped in a blanket
loving poetry and if no one ever recognized you
if there were no rooms
that would've been fine too and
you could've walked until you got to the city
of your birth, just for the hell of it,
just to see a dream-sickened ocean city
once, to come to the end of a rope, once,
to be able to turn
and look back at distance and duration
utterly transformed, and think
tonight the ugly ones could win, tonight the windows
could destroy the bricks, it must happen
sometimes otherwise everything goes on.
But you believed there
was tomorrow and tomorrow and tomorrow
for all that when there wasn't, and so you pushed and steered
the car onto the road, you and
your dead friend, and exited the pool
and grabbed a towel and drank a last drink and
left the dog beside the road, it was 1995
and you didn't know anything.

See Them

See them on the trampoline, her back garden,
shadow-shifting in the winter evening
as they jump and sit and jump again;

see them drive the night roads to the next bay
on a whim; see the dawn
a ribbon bridge in a snapping high wind;

see them bedded, see them move against
each other make their bodies give, in reach
the flammable mix of coral, moon, peach;

see them flail in the black wind
blowing at them, as they will again,
and again; see them still and see them fierce,
the heartfish bright in its bloodlight;

see them know they won't be leaving
by the same door they entered through,
whatever else they may not know;

see them also set against a bigger picture,
see them in history, all those oddly
mouthing figures in their guttering; all that dimming

colossity; see them with family, see their children;
and see them careful too
as though all this were a stone by stone

raging river hopping, some crossing
after many sleepless days and nights
that all depends on; and possibly they are right.

See them turn from the window, turn from the door,
to the old shards in the bowls back there,
which must get past the working throat,

they still think, but see them fling
all that across the room; see them use
what they have; see them use their hands;

see them hold each other better
though the sea always wins, not the house; and see
the full surprise of the untested

best of them's arrival; that day (and since)
the world was supposed to end
but didn't.

A Thing of Theirs

In a semiarid landscape,
where the speeches are done, where the wars
are over, a couple in a kitchen
work at a thing of theirs.

It occurs in the middle distance
but sometimes one can almost know their conversation.
See how he lights a cigarette for her,
briefly touches her hand before he lights his own.

It has been, sometimes,
like hauling a body across sand.
They have left the grander rooms to darkness.
See how they turn their heads.

In a slow-revealing landscape
they push aside the table and the chairs.
Move right there, showing no concern
for promises of arrival.

Ecstasy Revolver

Not that I know her well.
But not that she is not dangerous.

Dangerous like an ecstasy revolver.

She has unclever feet, that's the problem,
that's one problem,
a broken skewly healed neck,
back scars where they took
what they needed to fix her neck,
neck scars, too, of course.

You see how it is,
it's irresistible, if you then
also consider her eyes,
if you then also
factor in all other parts of her,
and her needing to be talked down from
trees and drawn to them
particularly incessantly.

I have tricks and stamina sure
but you need an axe and accidents
to make this work
the way it could.

You need to breathe
in stone, breathe out a flower, fearless.
You need to find who pays for the river
and pay for *them*.

I think you know what I mean.
This is a love poem.

She'll just laugh, say,
you can still change your mind buddy.
Her fingers already inside me,
her breath already in my language.

Nobody changes their mind.

Nobody doesn't want all of it.
The gun to the head at the end of it.

I write this in a room in summer.
South Africa. 2011.

You can turn around now, she says.

Sunnyside

At 1 a.m. he walks her home from the restaurant
where she works, unemployed himself, a student
nominally, happy to sleep in the morning and read
all day and walk through Sunnyside to get her

every night, past the children glued to the street and
the glass and vomit the fun-loving leave behind, a free
drink with the barman if she's still cashing up then back
holding her hand like a hero would, to their bedroom

with a window on the Union Buildings and the mattress
on the floor, candles wedged in bottles for atmosphere,
where she moves above him and makes her body yield,
or watches television without sound until it gets light, or

he does what he is best at, tries to make her laugh, stands
bug-eyed on the carpet pulling at his hair, turning in
circles, as he'd joked even when she first took him home
to where she lived with her mother, standing in the kitchen

waiting for the kettle, saying *I didn't know linoleum was still
permitted in the east*, for it was clear from the tangled garden
(here where mowing was the sport of kings) and the old
Nissan and the cat-piss smell of the carpets that someone had let

themselves go, was having problems as the saying goes,
though of course she didn't laugh, just gave him his coffee
and took him to her room and locked the door behind them
though no one else was home, *Poetry is braver than anyone* he would

say now if he was that young again and required to hold
someone young as him who needed what he wasn't sure he
had or could summon or could fake indefinitely, though the
line hadn't been written yet and her nakedness could neither

be carried nor put down, by him, and they got the flat in
Sunnyside, living broke and scared and hidden together,
and dancing some nights as though the end was to be seen,
in the two and a half clubs in that shitty city long-haired boy

faces were safe from getting smacked around in, talking always
of travel, neither of them having been anywhere, just talk,
sweet and inconsequential, until she went ahead and did it,
scrounged and saved for London and worked there in a fudge

factory and made it work, toughed it out, two months passed before
he vowed to save for airfare, for himself, which he didn't do.

Antarctica

I thought someone or something else
would also speak eventually

but it was just us. In time a candle and one
ration left and everywhere Antarctica.

We hadn't known we could travel so far.
I would've walked into the snow

but you did first.
Were we even right,

thinking one of us must?
Then I heard too many things,

then I moved as I had to,
to get back.

The whalers didn't recognize me,
you had not passed there.

I could not stop eating.
Unshockable stars. Unshockable ocean.

When I cannot find you
I give your name to everything.

1999

The first shock of cold does not surprise them,
but they move awkwardly even after that,
fitfully buoyant in the water, fearful now,
the late lesson beginning, and taught bluntly:

this water is not that water, that illicit
quarry swimming a decade ago in the dark,
the unforgettable shock of each other
utterly unclothed, the utterly altered land

that still betrayed them somehow, for
they are not those people now who knew everything
in 1999, when they knew nothing

but how to shake themselves from themselves
rather than half-float in pale gracelessness,
looking where sky would be.

Mourning for Beginners

—Jo

You have a jar of white feathers.

You water the garden at night
then let the garden go.

In a dream she asks you to dance
for her but you can't.

You say to yourself *This is how you do it*
as though you knew
how to do it.

You say it aloud as though that helps.

Alone you often speak aloud
being unsure of how she hears
and doesn't, where she is.

You don't know where she is, disappeared
as though she fell through a knife.

You wear her underwear.

You take the dog for walks but sometimes
you kick the dog too, anger
like a black space suit.

There is no manual.

Someone says *A difficult thing
is months later when you still
want to talk about it and friends don't.*

It has been some months.

You sleep with a rose quartz crystal
and a spade, one for the heart
and one for intruders.

You go thin and then you go fat.

There is a court case
but you ignore it, also twenty-seven shit-faced
behind a wheel plenty of times.

There are roses.

You put up more pictures, fix the
children's bedrooms, go with them
to the aquarium.

You say to a friend *I can almost work again.*
You say *I have good days and bad days.*

By now you have a special face
to go with that.

Things arrive in the mail.

The dog star rises above the patio rail
just as it did two years ago
when you moved here.

You burn the bridges as you cross them.

Self-Portrait as a Father

The aging fool with a fool's winning demeanor,
thinning hair, belly like a party balloon
days after the party,
who still believes, on his balcony,
in his jacuzzi, on his grunting back,
the sweet filth whispered in an ear,
his daughters with their mother on such nights.

Who can read at all hours in any place,
make from words a gravelly detour
to nowhere in particular,
his particular overly clever nowhere,
while still unknown the useful names of
garden plants and stars, the feeding patterns
of the owl and squirrel,
the simple shapes to draw a bunny looking like a bunny.

In other words (and for him there are
always other words) growing only older
exactly as his ex-wife said he would,
when they lived together still and the children
stared agape at such undoings.

Whose own parents did not know
what to make of him, living careful as Switzerland
through his upheavals and beratings,
who never wanted daughters
but hardly loved until he did,
hardly thought he'd be up at six to read the story,
again, of the boy and the penguin
not lost but lonely,

already fearing calls
he may have to take years from now at two in the morning,
that begin with a request to confirm
your name, the caller calling from a mess of
blood and metal or a public phone
beside a public park, something wholly beyond his indolent
abstraction, his endless fitfulness, fitlessness,
here where, reading history,
one would think there were no children.

Stone

Stone for water-skipping, stone for window-breaking,
stone for sharpening knives or to line a garden path,
a paperweight, a doorstop, a hidey home of insects,
stone that fits into a fist on a summer morning in a veld,
stone to clutch during field surgery, to build with, certainly,
and to suck in hunger, necklace stone framed by other shinier stones,
stone she said put to your lips, it's still warm from the sun,
that you painted at a children's party once,
that might still tell time if shadow fell across it right,
talking stone in marriage therapy,
stone for alley murder, sure, and for body- and boat-sinking too,
and to push bare-toed across the floor
repeatedly at the seeming end of the point of anything,
that could be traded for the useful things
were it not so common, that could be traded for
the longed-for things were it not so full of changing uses,
evasions, excuses; stone that fire and water,
applied in turn, could crack and split quite easily
like any stone.

With the Music Teacher

Some instruments, such as the one
you say you've chosen,
the one I teach, are really
best learned from an early age,
if bones are to harden awkward-angled
as required, if the needed breathing
is to be acquired. Close
to the memory of water (call it water)
you need not fear immersion, she said.
She said it may be too late for you
to make the hard journey down
repeatedly, return again and again
and sing of it convincingly,
to not hesitate, equivocate, give the game
away entirely, you who don't
look like a diver, a miner, a singer,
but rather (pardon me)
like a dabbler turned semi-desperate,
who thought once to force the ocean
through the eye of a needle
as others had, then not knowing
where or how to start, stood there too long,
afraid to pick a spot to stick it
when any spot would've done, around him
the storm enraging (call it storm)
and made a run for it
right here to me, calling cowardice
his own technique,
the flight his own fool song.

Rehearsal Notes

Sorry, I assumed you were awake anyway.

Let's try it without the heavy breathing
toward the end of the scene in the garden.
It distracts, somehow. Just speak the words, there
and elsewhere, as loudly
or as quietly as they need to be spoken.
Need in this context is vague, but do your best.
Don't get me wrong, subtlety is not the goal,
not on our budget, but an untested intensity
will flounder somewhere between the prompter
and the first row of the audience.
They know the story too, after all,
and it will be late by the time you face them.
Don't gaze into the distance when the
future is referred to. Don't hope
when you speak of hope.
Presumably it's not easy being us
but consider the alternatives.
Have you looked around recently?
In scene four you are passing an empty bowl around
that must seem heavy, but overdo
the heaviness and its emptiness is the final
lingering effect. Do you see what I mean?
I mean use the sharp knives carefully.
I mean real tears
don't mean you're acting well, just that you've lost
yourself in yourself again,
and where the script says scream
a step to the side and possibly a finger
touched to the mouth will do.

Jonah

I saw little there inside the whale,
barely heard the rush of water;
could not even guess at my place
in the oceans of the world.

But what a rigmarole, anyway,
just to end again in God's anger
and the telling of it
to farther cities of whimsy and gore,
who've heard it all before.

Nor was my body, then or later,
flayed to a pointed brilliance,
a golden song spewed forth.

At best, perhaps, my mind pulled
inside out, like the octopuses
caught and killed along the shore
by children of the fishermen.

I love what I cannot come to the end of.
The voice of God sometimes too much like my own,
sometimes like a wave in me.

Though really this work
has little to do with the sea.

In a Language That You Know

I could talk to you more
in a late language we both know,
I could believe no matter what you claim,

no matter how you change your story
or what you smell of, what places, long closed down,
you say you spent a quiet evening in.

Given half a chance I'd talk to you more
in the witless language of muck
and fervor, confusion and forgetting,

made less by what I lost
than what I became
in order to continue. It gets worse,

but I have my own hole to fill, and though
you haven't asked, yes
there's a fair amount of luck involved.

I could talk to you more
but you know by now
you can't take me anywhere.

Doctor

If the waiting room ambience
were better, perhaps it would be easier.

If there were more music, say,
or a bowl of mints
always on the counter, or if the lighting
were just dimmer.

The instruments he uses, vaguely
like instruments of torture
as we've seen them in films and museums
must have something to do
with our hesitation.

Engrossed, oblivious to all
but the shifting facts
of the particular case he goes to work,
when we make it in.

Almost cruel,
his focus. Small talk is discouraged.
He says he perfected his craft
in night school. He may be serious,
he may be joking
to put us at our ease.

We are told to breathe deeply, but can't.
We say we want this, we want that,
he looks up to say
want is a strong word.

Sending us on our way
he says hopefully we won't need to meet again,
and we agree, and resolve, brief
lightness in our step.

He sounds each time
as though he really means it.

Then the same road home
through the same flagless fields,
the rain in the dark,
the snapping to in the morning.

Yes doctor, it's me again, we say,
returning.
He says listen, and we do,
continues with his cutting.

Simple

I'd recognize you now
in an instant
yet I'd struggle to describe you to a friend
as you were then.

What mattered was
I was there to win you forever.

I had no other business to attend to
and knew it and everyone who
knew me knew it too.

Having won you
I'd speak no more of any of it,
I'd decided, but since I didn't
I haven't stopped.

ACKNOWLEDGMENTS

Some of the poems in this collection first appeared in *New Contrast, New Coin, London Magazine, A Look Away,* and on LitNet, as well as in the chapbook *Otherwise Everything Goes On* published by Slapering Hol Press in association with the African Poetry Book Fund and *Prairie Schooner.*

NOTES

COAST

The line "clever as orphans" derives from Margaret Atwood's prose piece, "Orphan Stories."

THE STOWAWAY

The line "a sky claimed in all its zones" derives from "I have taught you that the sky in all its zones is mortal" by Anne Wilkinson. I am familiar with it through Michael Ondaatje's *In the Skin of a Lion*.

ECSTASY REVOLVER

The lines "You need to breathe / in stone, breathe out a flower" derive from "It is time the stone made an effort to flower," by Paul Celan, in the poem "Corona," as translated by Michael Hamburger.

SUNNYSIDE

Sunnyside is a neighborhood in central Pretoria, the administrative capital of South Africa.

The line *"Poetry is braver than anyone"* is a misremembering of "Poetry, braver than anyone" by Roberto Bolano, in the poem "Resurrection," as translated by Laura Healey.

To order or obtain more information on these or other University of Nebraska Press titles, visit nebraskapress.unl.edu. For more information about the African Poetry Book Series, visit africanpoetrybf.unl.edu.

Lightning Source UK Ltd.
Milton Keynes UK
UKOW01f0018170817
307469UK00001B/23/P